THE C

Enhancing Your People Skills to

Increase Your Influence

DEDICATION

This book is dedicated to my three beautiful children, Dajhena, Kenyatta and Symphony, for without your love and support this would not have been possible. It is also dedicated to my best friend, Ivy; you are the reason why I am a Confident Leader and I love you always.

TABLE OF CONTENTS

Introduction

Have you ever met someone who can talk to just about anyone? How about someone you know who you can talk to about anything and they always seem to have the right kind of advice? Most would refer to them as a "people person" and this means that this particular person enjoys and is particularly good at interacting with other people. Plain and simple. In learning what it takes to be a confident leader, enhancing your "people" skills will help you increase your influence. What if you could just follow a few simple rules that would help you enhance your people skills and help you become a more confident leader? Just sit back, relax, and grab a cup of your favorite drink and you will learn how to become a confident leader through learning the people person model, catapulting your life to new heights that will have everyone wanting to be around you.

Hi, my name is Tameka Anderson and I have dedicated my life to helping parents, leaders, and businesses succeed by growing their "people-relations" skills. Let's face it; people are the heart of every business. They are our partners, competitors, management and staff.

But what if you knew how to relate to the people you did business with to the point where they were more like your friends? Friends help friends succeed in anything and everything. So how much would your business grow if you could merge your business relations with your people relations, more like becoming a people person?

Would you jump at the opportunity to learn the necessary tools you need to acquire great people relations skills and make them work for you?

Would you like to obtain clients who keep coming back mainly because they love doing business with you?

If you answered yes to any of the above questions then you are EXACTLY the person who needs to read this book. In the following chapters, I will share the six most important areas needed to obtain and maintain healthy and productive relationships. Then I will explain the six areas that every people person focuses on daily in order to relate to others on all levels. Lastly, we will cover the attributes it takes to increase your level of confidence as a leader. How you effectively relate to others could mean the difference between getting 100% of what you want out of life or struggling to get to the next step. Ultimately, people don't care how much you know until they know how much you care.

CHAPTER ONE
CONFIDENT LEADER VS. PEOPLE PLEASER

What is the difference between being a confident leader and a people pleaser? Is there any difference? Of course there is.

Let's talk about what it means to be a people pleaser first. Do you think you are a people pleaser? Ask yourself one question and answer it as honestly as you possibly can. When you do things for other people, do you often get angry with yourself for doing too much and never knowing how to say no? If you have answered yes to this question, sorry to break the news but you are definitely what we would refer to as a people pleaser. You have no say in anything that goes on in your life and look to others to tell you how to act, what to think, and even who to give to.

PEOPLE PLEASER

"There just isn't any pleasing some people. The trick is to stop trying." – Robert Mitchum

This disease is oftentimes viewed as something that can easily be cured, but most people need a little more assistance in this area. A people pleaser will do and say ANYTHING to please others and often gets taken advantage of. Only when they have been burned by enough people do they learn. By then they are unable to 'please' anyone anymore, especially themselves.

In some cases, being a people pleaser might be code for being codependent. Some people cannot seem to live or breathe unless they meet the approval of others, thus, depending on others instead of themselves.

When we put another's needs before our own, our energy is depleted, which can lead to depression, physical illness, and oftentimes overwhelm. This is what it means to be a people pleaser. People pleasing can also become so ingrained that it creates a victim mentality. People who give too much are susceptible to being taken advantage of, and resentment results.

If you've ever felt that resentment, you might think it is directed towards others. Yet, underneath, it's resentment towards yourself for giving away your power. If you're a people pleaser, chances are good that this behavior stems from your own insecurities, such as seeking completion and a sense of self-worth in your ability to take care of others. It's also known as being addicted to validation but, since this book is not about addictions, we shall carry on.

In order to get out of this mentality and stay out of it, you must look for other areas where you, personally, feel like you need to grow in terms of your social skills and character. Instead of being so dependent on how others view you, start asking yourself how you feel about you.

Before you do something for someone else, ask yourself this question: Why am I doing this? If this person does not reciprocate, will this anger me? If the answer is no, proceed because you are doing it simply because you want to and don't feel dependent on how the other person may feel about you one way or another.

CONFIDENT LEADER

In order to be a confident leader, you must first learn how to be a people person—not to be confused with people pleaser as we read previously.

In the words of Emily Deschanel, "I'm definitely a people person. I love socializing and being around people and having a good conversation."

Dictionary.com describes a people person as "an outgoing, gregarious person with good communication skills." Interesting. To go a little further into detail, a people person is someone who engages the people she meets wherever she may be. These are the people who speak to others in the checkout line at the store, those gathered around the water cooler at work, or classmates hanging in the hall at school. These are people who usually join clubs or social groups with the simple intention of enjoying being with the other members.

A people person is usually the life of the party whether going to a park, museum, ball game, or other activity in the company of others. Volunteers at charity events or other places tend to be people persons themselves, and this is a good venue for honing your own social skills.

Take up good manners. People generally prefer to interact with polite, well-mannered people. Keep up with the news and current events.

This is a fertile area for conversation topics.

Be well-groomed and tidy. People are inclined towards the company of other people who are reasonably clean and well-kept. There's a fine line between being a people person and being a people pleaser, and mistaking one for the other can be hugely detrimental.

TRANSITION FROM PEOPLE PLEASER TO PEOPLE PERSON

"The art of pleasing consists in being pleased." – William Hazlitt

Becoming aware of this behavior is the first step to healing it. If you think you're someone who tries too hard to please people, ask yourself the following questions:

•What am I trying to get by giving so much?
•What would happen if I stopped putting others before me?

Answer these questions honestly and fearlessly and see what feelings come up for you. As you review your answers, you'll come to find that hidden beneath your desire to serve others is a deep desire to feel good enough. Becoming truthful with yourself about your need to people please will help you begin the process of changing the behavior.

Next, become conscious of putting yourself first. Not by being selfish, but learning the proper balance of healthy self-love. If you do not have a healthy love for yourself, it will be impossible to either give or receive love from others. Repeat this phrase I coined: "It starts with me, if it's to be."

If your cup is not full, you will have nothing to give.

Self-indulgence is a radical act of self-care. At least once a day, do something kind for yourself. Cook yourself a meal, take yourself on a date, read a book, watch a movie, or whatever else you like to do. (To make it more fun, find ways you can treat yourself without spending money.) This may feel uncomfortable in the beginning, but it's important to create a new pattern of taking care of YOU first. You'll be surprised at the awesome results you will begin to experience, with a new wave of hope and love to spread around.

The next thing that you must do is start to create clear boundaries. If you're a people pleaser, more often than not, people expect a lot from you.

As you move into a new phase of your development, it's imperative that you begin to establish boundaries that feel comfortable for you. Simply start sharing with your friends, family, and others in your circle that you desire to develop a healthy love for yourself and you must take care of self first. Letting others in on your shifts will help them to help you.

Remember, there's nothing wrong with helping others, but your own physical, mental, and emotional health must come first. Learn how to say, "No." Don't make up excuses.

The most liberating thing you can do for your emotional well-being is to say no and simply give your reason(s). For example, if you don't want to be on the phone and someone calls you, simply let them know you do not desire to speak at this present moment. Unless it is a dire emergency (in which you are the only one who can assist) stand firm and don't allow yourself to feel bad.

Your best friend may want you to go with her on an outing. In addition to you being an introvert and knowing that you would not like the "scene", simply say, "No thanks, there are other ways that I can support you best and this is just not one of those ways." You don't have to be unkind. As a matter of fact, when you become emotionally independent you can be courageous and kind at the same time without giving in.

Start small by finding something little to say "no" to, and say it firmly. Say it politely, but mean it! You'll be surprised — the world will not collapse around your ears! People rarely take offense, and those who do aren't worth pleasing in the first place.

Ask for what you want. Part of getting out of the people pleasing habit is not always going along with the crowd, even standing out at times. For example, say you are with a group and you are deciding to grab a bite to eat.

Most people may say that they would like Chinese but you want pizza, by all means, speak up! It doesn't mean you get to have pizza, necessarily, but who knows—maybe there are others in that group who would prefer pizza as well, and were people-pleasing too! There's nothing wrong with voicing your opinion, and it doesn't have to mean you're making a demand. Simply reminding people that you're an individual with your own preferences is a big step forward.

Another thing you can do is ask someone to help you do something. You must remember that no one can read your mind. If you feel that you do so much for others, but they don't do anything for you, maybe it's because you don't express your needs or desires.

It's not fair to make people pry answers from you. If they ask you what you want, or if there's a decision being made, put in your opinion, and let that be that.

One major point people pleasers need to remember is to practice not worrying what anyone else thinks. Don't get caught up in doing things "their way" just because you don't want others to think badly of you. Also don't buy into others trying to manipulate you into not doing things "your way." Important fact: the most liberating thing is to take a stand.

"Never be afraid to take a stand, even if it means standing alone." –Tameka Anderson

Remember that there ought to be things that you truly want to do for yourself, regardless of what anyone else thinks, not in spite of it. Other people's opinions are a factor in our lives, but they should not be the determining factor.

COMPROMISE

"All compromise is based on give and take, but there can be no give and take on fundamentals. Any compromise on mere fundamentals is surrender. For it is all give and no take."

– Mahatma Gandhi

While it's not good to be a pushover, it's no better to be a manipulative bully or a reckless rebel. Don't become totally selfish. In fact, many people pleasers have low self-esteem. So do those who are selfish. It is best to develop good self-care skills, which include healthy assertiveness skills.

You can listen to others, but, ultimately, what you do is your choice. Keep a balance.

Sometimes the needs of other people should come first. Whenever there's a conflict of desires, try to come up with a solution that will meet both desires halfway, or, better yet, a "win-win" situation where both sides gain even more than they bargained for.

LONG-TERM SOLUTION

When you learn that being a people pleaser comes from a place of fear, if you wish to promote long-term growth, you must first examine your fears. Are they realistic? Are they truly terrible? You might be afraid that no one will like you, that someone will leave you, or that you will be left all alone if you don't say the right thing. That is a prison you have trapped yourself in, and it's time to unlock the doors and walk out. The truth is no one is guaranteed to stick around or even like you. When you embrace this fact, it will empower you.

Being a people pleaser, the people around you may be used to your compliance. But if they're not willing to accept that you have your own needs, are they really worth having in your life?

Evaluate your boundaries. Compare them to the limits you set on others. To what extent are you willing to restrict your openness to being used by others? What is acceptable behavior for you and what is unacceptable? Providing honest answers to these questions will help you to analyze your choices in a much more objective manner.

Always do what I like to call a "self-inventory", where you ask a series of questions to evaluate situations where you are feeling disturbed and/or disappointed. Ask yourself about the boundaries you set:

- Are you solid in what you ask of as well as give to others?
- Do you tolerate the intolerable?

- Normalize the abnormal?

- Accept the unacceptable?

- Do you know what it feels like to be treated with dignity and respect?

Learn how to identify and label unacceptable treatment from others and how to set limits on their behavior when they violate your boundaries. For example, if you have set a certain time of the day when you no longer take phone calls and someone continuously ignores your boundaries or makes you feel guilty about them, it may be time to sit that person down and tell them how they make you feel. If they listen, learn, and discard the behavior, keep them around. If not, remove them from your circle.

Remember the phrase, "Consider the source." Many people pleasers were raised in environments where their needs and feelings were pushed aside, not considered, or even belittled. Being able to identify and understand the source allows us to better understand ourselves, and to better eliminate our need to be a "people pleaser". Were you always expected to anticipate and mold yourself to everyone else's needs? Were you expected to shoulder the family's needs at a young age?

Did you learn that the only way to receive a positive response was to do what others wanted you to do? What would happen if you didn't do what they wanted, would they disapprove and berate you?

If so, newsflash — you being a pushover does not make you attractive to most people in the world. By focusing on pleasing others, you open yourself up to manipulation and abuse. You will never reach your potential as an individual if you constantly hide behind others' expectations. Eventually, when people have had enough of your services, they will not have recognized you for your true worth, but for the number of errands you could do for them.

One thing you must remember is to discontinue basing your self-worth on how much you do for other people. It's noble that you want to help others, but it's something you should do because you want to, not because you feel you have to. Your willingness to help others should come after you know how to help yourself. The greatest acts of kindness are those done by choice, not out of fear or guilt.

So that you can become aware of your behavior, ask yourself these questions before you do anything further for people:

Why am I doing this? Will I feel the need to let people know how much I have done for them? If I'm doing things for others because I would feel bad if I didn't, is my action really genuine? Would I want others to help me under those terms? And, if I'm helping others to such an extent that I am neglecting myself, is that really wise?

Some telltale signs that you're too entwined in the lives of others include: you are either passive or aggressive, with little or no give and take in between; you never seem to be having any fun; you are constantly controlling or being controlled; you are often in a hurry, usually for no reason. The reason these are some signs is because people pleasers usually have no balance so therefore everything is very extreme with them. When you find that your actions are being extreme (either to the left or the right) then this is a huge sign that something is wrong.

Never think that the world will collapse around you if you fail to please someone. If the "friend" you were trying to please leaves you because you did not please him or her then they were not your friend and it's good that they left. Know that there are always new friends to find. However, keep doors open just in case your friend realizes the mistake he or she made.

Be persistent. If this has been a lifelong habit, it will not be easy to overcome. Maintain enough self-awareness so that you realize when you are being a "pleaser", and put the brakes on it every time from this point forward. Eventually, it will become a habit that you can moderate when the situation calls for you to be more flexible. The rest of the time—have it your way.

Be yourself. How do you expect people to like you if they can't see who you really are? There is only one way for people to learn to like you and that is by showing them the person you are when you are alone, the person you know and love. This makes you true, original, and interesting. Be your own person, build your brand. You don't have to fit anyone's stereotype, maybe the real you is what they are looking for. Take the chance to get something you never had, to do something you have never done.

Don't blame others for your decision to change. Don't say, "I had to do this because of you." Remember that you are deciding to change for yourself. Some people may take time to adjust to the new you. Don't apologize for being you, but be gentle with them.

Some people may seem to reject the new, more assertive, less-of-a-pushover you. Some things to consider are that, yes, you may very well be afraid to change at first and others will be afraid and may not understand and reject the change.

Do not take this as a setback; just understand that those who do not have your best interest at heart will not want to be around you. But honestly, do you want them to be? Be patient with others who will see the new you and not reject it but may step back a little. They are simply trying to process the change.

Just as you were capable of understanding that change is nothing to fear, others will come to realize this in time. You can do much to

inspire people and calm their own
fears by resisting your own.

Our Deepest Fear

Our deepest fear is not that we are
inadequate.
Our deepest fear is that we are
powerful beyond measure.
It is our light not our darkness that
most frightens us.
We ask ourselves, who am I to be
brilliant, gorgeous,
talented and fabulous?
Actually, who are you not to be?
You are a child of God.

Your playing small does not serve the
world.
There's nothing enlightened about
shrinking so that other
people won't feel insecure around
you.
We were born to make manifest the
glory of
God that is within us.
It's not just in some of us; it's in
everyone.
And as we let our own light shine,
we unconsciously give other people
permission to do the same.
As we are liberated from our own
fear,
Our presence automatically liberates
others.

—Marianne Williamson

The ability to express your own desires first requires your awareness of what they are, which requires conscious and consistent practice. For example, a friend or family member may suggest that you go grab some pizza and you may really think, *Yeah, okay, I guess that is cool.* It is only "cool" because you never make that choice; you never actually decide what you would like to do. Take the few extra seconds to consider it. Ask yourself a question; where would you go instead if you were alone? Tell them that's where you would like to go this time.

As with anything in life, you must practice the appropriate response for each situation.   For example, you may not want to get tattoos on your face if you work in a corporate setting, because you do not want to lose your job. At times, only pleasing yourself may not be appropriate. Sometimes you need to compromise.

An example of a compromise is if you are in a committed relationship with another person and this particular person enjoys the outdoors but you do not. Sometimes, it is appropriate to accommodate your significant other in order to show that person you are not only interested in yourself but also in doing what pleases them. This is a way of pleasing people sometimes.

Try to please people sometimes.

CHAPTER TWO

WHY BECOME A PEOPLE PERSON?

"I'm a people person, very approachable. I go out every night, tons of functions. I love all facets of this industry... Music, film, TV, books, art. I love being around creative people."

– Guy Oseary

One of the main points most people tend to agree on in both the corporate world and in public service is that a people person achieves greatness. This is a person who is usually a leader of industry and of government. When a CEO appears on the news or a talk show, more often than not, that person is a good communicator and has charisma. Just think about President Barack Obama. Despite everything people may say or think about him, one thing they cannot dispute is that he definitely is a people person.

Likewise, politicians win office in many cases, not on the merits of their track record, but because they have charisma or a good "television face".

Once again, President Barack Obama wins this argument.

A Confident Leader Is a People Person

The ability to relate well to others is a great indicator that you will be successful in any and all arenas especially when it comes to the professional world. You could have the greatest talents in the world and be the most brilliant, but without the necessary social graces, you most likely will not develop into a leader or trailblazer. People who best relate to others make it big in this world. This is a proven fact, so it would be wise to focus on relating to others as much and as often as possible. In addition to the other valuable tools in their skill set, from connections and education to experience and money, it is a powerful indicator of success.

For every great leader, there are millions of other people with drive and promise who cannot get their message across. They lack something very important—interpersonal skills. The term has many connotations in the context of career and professional life. Plain and simple what this means is the ability to empathize and relate to people to elicit genuine rapport and great favor. How you both behave and relate in social settings is one thing, how you behave in your career setting is another.

But if you possess great interpersonal skills, you begin to tie everything in together and become a force to be reckoned with.

Interpersonal skills are life skills we use every day to communicate and interact with other people. People with strong interpersonal skills are usually more successful in both their professional and personal lives. Learning how to relate to others is a very important tool necessary for growth and development.

Employers hope to hire people with strong interpersonal skills. They want people who work well in a team environment and are able to communicate effectively with coworkers and clients. People with good interpersonal skills are usually perceived as optimistic, calm, confident and charismatic, which are qualities that are often seen as appealing to others.

Listed below are some brief telltale signs of a confident leader:

Confident Leaders Listen

Some leaders hear, while others listen. Then there are those who listen in an active sense. Active listening includes not only listening without interrupting someone, but listening to understand. If you have to ask more questions, do so. They are the great leaders you want to follow. When people speak, do you find yourself thinking of what you want to say or, even worse, do you interrupt others while they are speaking?

Confident Leaders Are Focused

Are you the type of person who listens in detail when people speak?

Do you catch every word as if you are a wordsmith? Do you pick up on emphasis, intonation, body language, and facial expressions? Great leaders focus well in conversations. Call them observant if you will. Be observant not just of the words, but how they are being said. This is something great leaders do very well.

Confident Leaders Connect

Confident leaders become great simply because others deem them as such. One of the ways they are great is with their connecting to people. Confident leaders communicate a message to each person they connect with that everyone is important. In order to make someone feel important, you must maintain eye contact with them and give them your undivided attention. Something as simple as making eye contact helps you connect with people. When you fail to make eye contact, you come across as aloof, unsympathetic and arrogant. Most people take this for granted. But watch the great ones, because nine times out of ten, their eyes are watching you.

Confident Leaders Empathize

The ability to put yourself in another person's shoes and feel what emotional state another may have been in is essential to build rapport. Can you relate to their personal life experience? Do you care about them as a person? Confident leaders genuinely care about all people, no matter what. It is as simple as that. Compassion and sensitivity are the key components of a successful people person. It is imperative that you exercise both when you relate to others.

A Confident Leader Is Successful

As we already established, being a people person has absolutely nothing to do with being a people pleaser and it also has nothing to do with being a push-over. Not at all. It's actually a method of recognizing and connecting with the moods of the people around you. For example, in a discussion at work, be mindful of the frame of mind and disposition of those in attendance.

When you have knowledge of how someone else is feeling, this allows you access to see how you as a person can be of service to them; it opens the door to connecting with people even more. This is a huge advantage in both business and personal life. When you connect with people it's easier for you to do things like negotiate terms, attempt to drive a point home, or even make an unpopular decision. When you take time to become a people person and hone your interpersonal skills, you can work with and gain access to some invaluable resources—co-workers, clients and/or management.

The problem is that most people seldom take the time to hone what is, in essence, a critical skill to attain both personal and career development.

If having great interpersonal or people skills is so critical to success, and most people say they want to be successful, why do we neglect honing our people skills? One of the main reasons is ego. We are egotistical by nature. Most people experience spurts of benevolence, but, overall, most look out for no one but themselves. This is not said from a negative perspective, it is merely a fact. The outcome of our self-absorbed behavior is that we shut off personal contact with others. Our focus is on our bottom line and what we can do to attain it. Something most people don't realize is when we take the time to relate and understand those around us, our end goals quickly fall into place, faster and quicker than if we were to do it alone. Being a people person makes you a successful person.

Interpersonal relations development is not just about our attention to the moods of others around us, but also to our own positive moods. This is where self-awareness comes in to play. A people person is successful not only at paying close attention to the mood and behavior of others but of themselves as well. Be mindful of your mood at all times. Negative emotions like aggression, anger, temper, baggage, and sometimes pessimism happen, just keep them away from others.

Good interpersonal skills start with you.

When you take a look at yourself what do you see? How is your facial and body language? What message are you sending others? If you don't know the answer to these questions, take some time and ask others what message your body and facial expressions display. When people tell you the message you're sending, believe them. For the most part, people will tell you how they feel if you ask them. Even if you have been a bit standoffish, cold, and/or distant, start today and decide on becoming a good people person with a positive attitude. You cannot control the moods of others, but you can control your own temperament. When you do, articulating a clear and positive message, this will push you to great success; people will want to do for you just because they like you.

A Confident Leader Has a Magnetic Personality

When you are a people person, one of the greatest benefits is that you become a human people magnet. People naturally want to be around you, do what you do, and learn what you know. This works to your advantage because you begin to develop such a bond with people that people will naturally want to move Heaven and Earth just by you saying the word.

If becoming a people person is one of your goals (given the reasons listed it definitely should be, but I digress), you can follow some basic points on how to act like a friendlier, more social person.

Understanding what it means to be friendly should be the first rule of thumb. A generic definition is to be nice to, and interested in other people. Being social means spending some time with other people and enjoying it. Notice I didn't specify how much time, but we will get into that later. Now, when you spend time with people do you genuinely enjoy it?

Most of the information presented speaks about the behavior you should display. If you have a personality where you enjoy people and are interested in everyone, many of the actions mentioned will come naturally. Developing into a people person, especially given the society we live in now, is easier said than done. However, regardless of how you're feeling, you can still discipline yourself to carry out these friendly and social behaviors.

The next point I would like to make is please do not become a phony, needy, or over-the-top 'friendly' person because most people can pick up when you are not genuine. These suggestions are merely a guide to keep you on the right track. Just maintain more self-awareness of your interactions with others. Two different people with two totally different personality types can still be considered people persons, yet maintain their sense of individuality.

If you are finding it hard to be more social and friendly without losing your own voice and personality, below are some things you could possibly try:

Start conversations with new people

This world is filled with people. Unless you live underneath a rock and don't ever interact with people (in which case how in the world did you get this book, right?), you are bound to meet new people from time to time. Let's say you are in the post office waiting in line to mail a package. If there is a long line that is more than a five minute wait, start a conversation with someone. Even saying, "Hi," asking for their name, and going, "Cool, nice meeting you. Hope to see you around these parts again soon," can be good. Remember, just use your own voice and let it shine.

Become approachable

Have you ever tried striking up a conversation with someone you've run into, and they blew you off by giving one-word responses and obviously looked like they didn't want to talk to you? Come on, you can tell the truth here, how did it make you feel? If you are anything like me, it probably made you feel kind of awkward, something like a stalker, right? Well, let me tell you a story.

I was called to be on set of a movie and I saw a tall, young woman. I walked up to her and simply said, "Hey, how are you?" Almost without giving me a second look, the woman mumbled something and walked away to sit on a bench nearby. Guess what I did? You are absolutely right; I took a seat right next to her. I felt like if I was going to be spending almost a half a day with someone, at least I was going to find out why she didn't want to talk to me.

Long story short; come to find out this young lady thought I was a threat to her position because I was called in to replace her on the set. After understanding her position, I quickly reassured her that I didn't want her spot, secured her, and she became a chatty Cathy after that.

The moral of the story is, had I been unapproachable, that would have been a hostile environment to work in. Anyone who has ever worked on set of a movie knows you could be there anywhere from 12 to 16 hours.

How awful would that experience had been if I'd brushed her off? Yikes.

Keep in touch

Haven't heard from someone in a while? Guess what, they say the phone line goes two ways (and in some cases three and four ways), so reach out and call someone just to keep in touch. Catch up with what they've been up to lately, or just talk about whatever. Maintain your relationships and show you're interested in other people. Most of us are so consumed in our own personal affairs that we tend to forget to reach out and touch someone (no I am not plugging another company, just happen to like the slogan).

Another thing that boils my blood is when people feel the only time they can contact you is when they need or want something from you. How would it make you feel if someone only contacted you when they wanted something? If you are human, it would make you feel used and unappreciated. So don't treat others like this even when you meet people who may treat you this way. Plain and simple, reach out and chat with someone just because you care.

Be inclusive

There is nothing worse than being the type of person who is exclusive. I know when you hear that word you probably say, "Hey, exclusive is the only way to be, right?" Bunch of bull and a load of crock. There are some people who feel it makes them seem more important by only having a "select" group of people they publicly acknowledge. How phony is that? Again, put yourself in that other person's shoes. How would you feel if someone treated you as if you didn't deserve to breathe the air they breathe, much less be in their circle?

Make an effort to bring new people into your circle and make them feel included. Allow people to be themselves and trust that you will find out quickly whether or not they deserve to stay in your inner circle. But we shall discuss that later. If you're out with some friends and there's a new person there, take the time to talk to them a bit, instead of being distant. Yes, is it awkward meeting new people but, hey, be yourself and if they don't like you, it's not the end of the world.

Be where people are

If your co-workers are going out for lunch, tag along. If they all eat lunch at a certain time and place then eat lunch at that time too. A huge part of being a people person is showing people that you actually like people. Remember people make the world go round (I know, I know, I gotta stop it). Show people that you want to spend time with them. Join in conversations when you are around people. Don't hang back and get lost in your head.

Talk to everyone, everywhere, about everything

If you can put it in your mind to talk to everyone, everywhere, about everything, there is a greater chance that you will grow your network of friends and supporters simply because you will show people that they matter; that you are willing to listen and join in conversations that not only matter to you but to them as well.

Spend time with people more often. Spend time with them longer. Spend time with more of them. For example, look at where you spend most of your time during the day and if you find that you spend most of your time at work, make it a challenge to talk to everyone, everywhere, about EVERYTHING.

You could be listening to someone have a conversation about puppies. Even if you don't have a puppy, find a way to join the conversation. You can even make a point of explaining why you don't own a puppy, even if that means you are not a "dog person" but are a "cat person".

Just as making a point of talking to more people can be challenging, you can also become overwhelmed by being around people too often. Life is about balance and having a healthy balance is what being a people person is all about. You must make a habit of not only carving out times to be around people, but also time to spend alone. You need time to decompress from all of the cognitive activity we put our brains through from engaging with people throughout the day.

Be nice to people

Ever heard the term, "Chivalry is dead"? Well, I would like to also go on record to say the act of people being nice to other people seems to be slowly dying. Help to revive this dying breed and do basic things like hold doors for people. Speak to people when you make eye contact with someone. The very least you could do is smile. You have no idea how far a simple smile will get you and allow people to break down their walls and barriers. It also boosts your people skills.

Do you like compliments?

If someone gave you a compliment, how would that make you feel? You would probably feel pretty good. So make a point to offer compliments to others. Challenge yourself to do the 5-second look over in which you take 5 seconds to look someone over from head to toe. Pick out at least one thing that you like about them, and then TELL THEM even, and especially, when someone seems unapproachable. When you offer a compliment, it helps to break down even the strongest wall.

Consider others always

Being a people person means you always consider others. Therefore, no matter where you go, you are more often than not considered the life of the party. Another trait of a people person is to always look for ways to include everyone in what you are doing. If someone seems left out of the conversation, try to maneuver it to a topic they can contribute to.

If someone seems like they want to say something, but they can't get a word into a lively discussion, casually indicate to everyone that they want to talk. If you're doing an activity that someone doesn't seem comfortable with, try to coax them to join in, if it's harmless and you know they'll have fun once they start. Or take some time to explain the basics to them if they aren't familiar with how to do it. If someone seems bored, or annoyed, see if you can somehow get them to have fun.

Are you the person who is so friendly that everyone who meets you instantly likes you? When you go to a party, are you friends with the entire room within a short time? If so, you are a people person. You are someone who is nice and has so much charm that others will do anything for you.

Earn trust and respect from others

If you are a people person, you are successful because you know how to earn trust. Other people are always willing to help. The more you give, the more you get and you never run out of assistance. If you are confident of your skills in a social setting and how to make the best use of them, you are empowering yourself.

Finding the power in your life will result in being more joyful and more successful. If you are not one of these people, but you want to know how to start, here is a list of ways to begin.

- Don't be ambiguous. People who like to "leave others in the dark" are seen as untrustworthy. Do yourself a favor, if you are uncomfortable talking about something, just say it but please don't avoid straight talk.

- Respect others' time. I get it;
  life happens but be sure to be
  the type of person who
  maintains an image of being
  prompt. If you are running
  late, call, just be respectful. In
  order to get respect, you must
  give it first.

- Answer questions without
  being defensive. If someone
  knows that if they are honest
  you will be defensive, this
  makes people feel like they
  can't be honest with you and,
  therefore, they will not trust
  you.

- Be accountable for your
  actions. This cannot be stressed
  enough. We are all human and
  make mistakes. When you are
  the type of person who can say,
  "I'm sorry," this builds trust
  and respect that will take you
  far in relationships.

CHAPTER THREE

READING PEOPLE

"When someone shows you who they are, believe them the first time."
– Maya Angelou

I love quotes (as you can tell from this book), but there are some authors I favor over others. Maya Angelou happens to be one of my most favorite poets. Her words just seem to flow like oil and smooth as butter. So when I first heard the quote about people showing you who they are, I really did not understand it. But the more I began to grow myself as a person the more the quote became second nature to me.

Learning to read people is another skill of a people person. Why do you need to learn how to read people? Simply because you need to know how you can reach and/or help them. If you don't know what someone needs, how can you be of assistance? At the end of the day, helping others is what being a people person is all about.

Learning how to read people

There are three basic areas in learning to read people:

1. Observation—visual area. Watch closely what the body language is saying to you.

2. Communication—listening area. Use active listening; people naturally like to talk about themselves, so let them talk and just listen.

3. Interpretation—consistency area. Comparing what is said, what is not said, and the body language is the only way to notice consistencies and inconsistencies.

You don't have to be an FBI interrogator to figure out what's going on in someone's head or to read people. The signals are always there, you just must be aware. You have to know what to look for and understand how to hear what is said and done. Keep in mind there's no single surefire way to tell what someone is thinking—even the greatest mind-wizards in the world are only right 80% of the time.

One of the first ways of learning to read people is just by having a conversation with that person. Something I have noticed about people is they like to talk about themselves. Therefore, starting a conversation with someone in which you ask them questions will get the process started. You are simply trying to observe a person's habits over time. A seemingly innocent question such as, "How are you doing today?" can start the conversation. Look for inconsistencies between the person's gestures and words.

If the person states they are fine, watch their body language. Are they moving around uncomfortably? Are they looking away when they say it? Usually, when we are trying to deceive others, we say one thing but inwardly something else is going on;

our body will move in an unnatural way when this happens. So if you notice that a person says they are "Fine," their body may say "something is wrong". Something as simple as touching them on the shoulder and saying, "I am here if you want to talk," will catapult you in the relationship because now you care about them as a person and they will begin to trust you.

If you are someone who feels unable to read people, here are some tips that may help:

Ask questions

Vague, open-ended questions don't work, because if the person rambles on, it becomes difficult to detect any deception. Instead, ask questions that require a straight answer. And don't be intrusive. After asking a question, sit back and observe without interrupting.

Observe the words people use

If someone says to you, "I bought another house," the word clue "another" conveys the notion that the person had previously purchased one or more houses. This person wanted to ensure that other people know that he or she bought at least one other home, thus bolstering his or her self-image. This person may need the adulation of others to reinforce his or her self-esteem.

Observe body language

Notice how the other person's body language is speaking to you. Are they calm and relaxed or do they seem anxious and tense? Do they look you in the eyes when speaking or look away? What are they doing with their hands?

Pacifying gestures such as touching the forehead or the rubbing of palms against thighs are indicators of stress.

Facial clues of distress and discomfort include the furrowing of the brow, clenching of the jaw, lip compression, or the tightening of face and neck muscles.

Ask why

One of my favorite questions, hands down, is "why?" Some people may not like it, but I have come to embrace it. If you are going to be good at reading people, you will need to learn to embrace this question as well. Asking someone why they did, said, or reacted the way they did will empower both of you. It will empower that person, because you are listening to them voice their concerns as opposed to forcing your own reasoning upon them. You will become empowered because hearing from them helps you read them better.

One of the greatest ways to read people is by asking very direct questions. Understand when you do this you will turn off those who make it a habit to be deceptive. Being around you will be very uncomfortable for them—that's okay because that's what you want anyway. Remember, we are people persons not people pleasers. So sometimes you will make people angry as a people person, especially when you read them like a book.

So how do you ask direct questions? First you must start with the basics. When you get people to talk about themselves, it becomes easier to ask them more direct questions. A direct question would be, "What do you hope to accomplish from our conversation today?"

Although this approach does catch people off guard, it will also allow you to read the true intention of the other person.

Another one of my favorite direct questions is, "What do you want from me?" I cannot tell you the response I get from others and how it makes me laugh when I ask that question. For some reason, we are living in some sort of illusionary world where most people like to beat around the bush.

So when you have people who are very open and direct, most people don't know how to respond.

As with everything, you must use direct questions in moderation. I usually tell people I will use direct questions on those who seem to be very ambiguous or unclear in their communications. For some reason, someone thought it would be a great idea to promote ambiguity. But I am here to tell you if you would like to be successful at being a people person, being ambiguous will get you nowhere.

So how do you know when someone is practicing the art of ambiguity? Easy. When you ask questions, are the answers very vague or so diluted that you are still lost as to what the real answer is? This is a huge indication that they are being ambiguous. One thing that I have learned from people who practice this art is that they are usually trying to hide or cover something up and cannot be trusted. Therefore, I stay away from them as much as possible.

Is it possible for a people person to not like certain people? Absolutely. When you have people who intentionally do not allow you to know their real self, this is someone who doesn't make a good people person candidate. More often than not, people who keep such a huge bubble around themselves are self-absorbed and unable to understand the social order of life. Therefore you cannot really establish a relationship with these people.

Manipulators and people who are ambiguous communicators are those who have mastered the art of deception; you cannot build productive relationships with them. You should be able to see how learning to read people is an important skill to gain as you continue to become a great people person.

Reading romantic cues

Does the same rule apply when reading someone who may be romantically interested in you? Here is a funny story. There was a young woman who just couldn't understand why, after dating guys for a while, all of a sudden they would seem very disinterested. "I just don't understand," said the young woman. "I meet men all of the time. We go out, I think everything is good, then all of a sudden he just stops calling. What am I missing here?"

Her best friend looked at her lovingly and responded, "Sweetie, I told you that you need to stop talking so much. When you're always talking, you miss all of the signs of the man and therefore get yourself in these situations." In a sense, her friend is correct. In order to read another person, you must be actively listening as well as watching. People tell you exactly what you want to know if you pay close attention.

The body language of flirting is elemental and hardwired within humans. Yet sometimes it's difficult to know whether someone definitely wants you, might possibly want you, wants you as a friend, or is just a nice person who would even show kindness to a statue. Specifically, a man may not be interested in a serious relationship with a woman, but this same man will go to the mountaintop if there's a possibility it may lead to a sexual experience.

Women, on the other hand, being more emotional creatures, will probably visualize how their children may look, what side of the bed he will sleep on, and whether or not he has a nice family before they even go out on the first date. That being said, oftentimes it is more difficult for a woman to read a man for whom she may have romantic feelings.

Men and women seeking to improve their dating ratio can start by keeping an eye out for some of the behaviors that people automatically display when they are really into each other. Most people, when they have a romantic interest, will use body language to send messages while speaking to you, just be sure to tune in.

For example, a man may draw attention to himself with a loud laugh or by spreading his arms wide. Both men and women might flash a broad grin, showing all their teeth. Once a conversation begins, some women slip into what men like to refer to as their "bedroom voices", while men may drop theirs an octave. As interest accelerates, flirters tend to mimic each other's stance and movements. And, finally, they make physical contact.

If, after a skillful sizing up of the situation, you still make the wrong call, the person you thought was falling for you turns red and stumbles away after you invite them to dinner, hold your head high and own your error. It may not have been an error on your part, but on the part of the other individual misleading you, whether intentionally or not. Therefore, owning your part in the situation helps to keep you accountable and gives you loads of confidence to boot.

Reading difficult people

"Okay, so not quite sure what just happened here?"

In the past, you've probably walked away from an exhausting exchange at your place of work, a party, in the grocery store, or with someone in your neighborhood, wondering whether you or the other person was to blame for a failed conversation.

Sometimes a chat goes astray because someone just doesn't seem interested in what you have to say or, conversely, doesn't let you get a word in edgewise. Other times, you might say something that was intended as harmless only to have your conversation partner misinterpret it and begin judging you harshly. An exchange can rapidly spiral downward if you sense the other person doesn't like you, resulting in you feeling the same way. Whether the encounter ends in feigned politeness or deadly silence, you're left confused or upset.

One of the most important things you should understand is that not all people are created equally. Some people are plain out difficult. They may not like what's going on in their life. They may be going through a lot of stress and rejection and would like to deflect those negative feelings on to you. When you learn how to read when someone is being difficult, it makes your life much better.

You can begin reading a difficult person by simply observing their posture first. Oftentimes, difficult people are not as easy to read as others. Unfortunately, it is not until that person speaks that you will truly understand whether or not they are difficult. One thing to do is to get them talking so you can assess the situation. The great thing about difficult people is you can usually read them a lot faster if you get them to talk to you. Will the encounter be uncomfortable? Probably. But keep your composure so that you can make an accurate reading and understand how to proceed.

When trying to understand people, you must take everything into consideration. An uncomfortable exchange might alternatively be the result of two clashing personalities. Sometimes people's values are simply incompatible. You may say something totally innocent, yet be grossly misunderstood. Each of you may miss the other's underlying motivation, intention, or innuendo. And neither party may feel the freedom to openly address the problem.

If someone you don't know well seems to be amusing himself with put downs, racial slurs or other blatantly offensive remarks, excuse yourself and walk away. Save your conversation for someone deserving of it. But don't write off a quiet person as aloof or cold; instead, assume they just need a little extra help. Dialogue isn't always fifty-fifty; sometimes the people person needs to carry more weight by asking questions, putting the other at ease, and giving sincere compliments to get positive feelings flowing.

In situations where it's to your advantage to befriend someone, don't develop a victim's mentality over one bad interaction. Let your curiosity guide you towards common ground, and become more complimentary towards that other person. There is ALWAYS something nice you can say about anyone. This compliment, in turn, may dispel any bad impressions he or she may have formed about you.

If you really can't tell whether someone dislikes you or if your encounters with this person seem forced and insincere, it's worth asking with care, "I'm sorry, did I offend you somehow?" If a misunderstanding has occurred, the well-intentioned person will rush to clear it up. When you have the courage to confront someone, you increase your skills and confidence in reading and understanding others.

Reading the "control freak"

There is a difference between manipulation and persuasion. A control freak uses many devices to manipulate others into doing/saying what they want; a people person uses the power of persuasion to inspire others. Both people try to get others to "buy in" to what they are selling; but the people person doesn't use deception as the control freak does.

Something amazing about a control freak is they have an amazing ability to "control" any and everything within their reach, everything except themselves. How do you read the control freak in order to be able to socially relate to them?

One thing about people who tend to be addicted to control is they seem to lack a certain amount of control over their life. This is perhaps the reason they want to have control everywhere else. More often than not, people who are control freaks use more manipulation than persuasion. The thing about manipulation and its kissing cousin, "control", is that they can influence individuals with or without their consent.

One can easily read a control freak by observing their body language and listening to their conversation. These people tend to be a tad insecure and it can be heard when listening closely. They say things like, "I know you think…" or "You should be saying…" The bolder control freak will even go so far as to say, "I do this or that for you…" These are telltale expressions that this person is trying to control how you think, a.k.a. manipulation.

Understand that the control freak lacks control and needs to feel some form of power over something. This is the only way to relate to them. If you have to deal with someone who is a control freak, allow them to speak as much as possible during conversations. This sends a message that they are important and have a level of control. At the same time, you may want to limit the interactions you have with this person because they will consume your emotions if you allow them to.

Because control is wrapped in manipulation, and manipulation manifests itself in conversations, these interactions must be closely monitored. When you have someone who is trying to gain power over you, they will stop at nothing to get what they ultimately want—which is control. This can be a huge emotional weight, so when you read into someone and they spell control freak, keep your distance!

CHAPTER FOUR

INTERPERSONAL RELATIONS

"I'm more interested in interpersonal relationships - between lovers' families, siblings. That's why I write about how we treat each other." – Terry McMillan

Think back to everyone you consider a people person. How does this person make you feel? Do you like to be around that person? Would you want to learn all you could from this person? If so, what is it about that person that just makes you smile?

These are the necessary ingredients to achieve success within interpersonal relationships:

- Communication

- Care & Consideration

- Commitment

- Conflict Resolution

- Control

- Consistency

"Communication" is the main ingredient in any relationship. Without it, the relationship will be very difficult to attain and maintain. "Care and consideration" are next; they're just as important ingredients because people don't care how much you know until they know how much you care. "Commitment" is another area. This goes without saying because, to achieve any great accomplishment, you must have an appropriate level of commitment to it.

The next ingredient is not a very popular one but, nevertheless, it's one you must master; it is "conflict resolution". This is necessary to maintain what you have already attained.

The penultimate ingredient is "control"—self-control. Without self-control, any efforts made or hurdles overcome can be destroyed in the blink of an eye. You MUST concentrate on the other ingredients first in order to even be able to attain this one. In order to learn how to control yourself, you must be able to master the other ingredients first then this one becomes easier.

The last ingredient is "consistency". It is last because it cannot be accomplished until all of the other ingredients are in place. It is also important because this process begins and ends within you. Being consistent requires self-discipline and focus in your mind and this is a major reason why most people will not consistently follow a diet. Everything starts in your mind. You know the saying goes, "Where the mind goes the man follows," so therefore you start in the mind then add some discipline and consistency is sure to follow.

The first thing you want to do in any relationship is establish a means of communication. In order to accomplish your goals, you must be able to clearly communicate your thoughts, dreams and desires to your prospective customers or clients. You must decide which methods of communication are most effective in your relationship and use the methods that work best for you. Clarity of meaning is very important in communication. Without clarity YOUR RELATIONSHIP WILL FAIL!

I am the type of person who really dislikes misunderstandings, both mine and other people's. I do not like to misunderstand people nor do I want to be misunderstood; I would prefer to conduct all my communication through email or text message because you will be able to actually read what I say in black and white. It leaves very little room for confusion. While that may work best for me, it may not be the best plan of action for everyone.

Establishing your most effective communication tool is so important because confusion can cause a major strain on the relationship.

You must keep in mind that some people may interpret the written word differently from the way you intended! So for those people, I make a mental note to make a phone call or even do face-to-face communication when the topic of discussion is too important to be left open to interpretation.

The reason it's important to recognize and establish your most effective communication tool is because confusion and miscommunication can cause a severe strain on the relationship as well. Never forget that misinterpreted or miscommunicated words, thoughts, or ideas can hurt feelings and permanently destroy a relationship! Being clear, concise, and convincing is important in making the most out of any relationship.

Another area you must fully understand is learning the difference between speaking and listening. Before you start laughing, you would be SURPISED how many people are not effective communicators because they do not know how to listen. Listening is twice as important as speaking—this is the reason I believe God gives us two ears and one mouth!

In becoming more effective, you should ALWAYS do what I call the "2 to 1". That means you should LISTEN twice as much as you speak. For example, if you are speaking for 5 minutes, you should listen to the other party for at least 10 minutes.

Even the shyest person will figure out how to communicate if you truly show your care and concern, but we will get into that later.

Remember that communication is both verbal and nonverbal; meaning what you say and what you do NOT SAY are almost equally important. For example, a hand gesture, a body movement, a frown, heavy breathing, even averted eyes are all nonverbal means of communicating. So be careful of these behaviors so that both types of communication are in agreement with what you intend to say.

"People may not always remember what you said, but they will always

remember how you made them feel!"
– Maya Angelou

Now please listen closely to what I will say next because this one thing will make or break a relationship, both personal and professional. R-E-S-P-E-C-T. This is an absolute MUST in every conversation because if you have no respect for the other person, you will subconsciously shut down and not hear what is said. In addition, this will cause you to speak ineffectively causing confusion within the conversation. Remember what I stated about how confusion can cause a strain on relationships? People have an extra sense and can feel when the respect is not there. This should be your mantra that plays on a continuous loop in your head: "I may not 'like' you, but I will RESPECT you!"

Let's be very honest here. If you are trying to establish a relationship then obviously there is a reason for you to be interacting with this person. They have something that you want. Respect THAT. Be honest and sincere in respecting their position.

I am sure I don't have to tell you all about the saying that goes, "People don't care how much you know until they know how much you care," and this is the entire truth. Showing care and consideration for another individual sounds simple, but you would be surprised at how much people get lost in this translation just trying to make another sale.

In my Confident Leader Seminar, I break down all of the proper steps of showing concern for another person and also clear signs when you it's working. Being sincere also sounds elementary but you have no idea how getting caught up into making a sale numbs your sincerity.

Sometimes people cannot relate to their superiors simple because they cannot relate. Simple as that. If you were to become transparent for one moment you will break more ground with others who may feel inferior in the relationship. For example, supervisors and managers will be able to gain a lot more ground if they understand the importance of relating to their subordinates. Something as simple as asking how they are doing and finding something that you can relate to will help build the gap in any superior/inferior relationship. Respect, ah here is this word once again. Respect is a VERY important factor in caring about another individual.

During the commitment stage of any relationship, if you are unclear of your role you will not know what role to play. Therefore, you will do one of two things: 1) Play a role that does not suit you or 2) Do nothing. Either way, it is a relationship drainer. Once you understand your role, you can perfect your role. I go into deeper depth of learning how to perfect your role in any relationship.

The key point here is commitment. You MUST and I cannot stress this enough, you MUST become an expert team player. Some people say they are a team player but seeing how actions speak louder than words, nothing about their actions spells "TEAM". I show you how to do a little exercise to test your team player skills.

As in every relationship, there will be some times where you want to quit and throw in the towel. Sticking in there during these times shows your level of commitment; obviously you must first define whether or not the relationship is worth sticking around or not. Of course, here is the idea of respect once again. When you respect each individual you respect their differences in opinion. It does not always have to be your way. More than likely, you won't always get 100%. Most of us are used to this anyway. However, there is always a compromise.

I must say this is my favorite portion of the book. At some point and time in any relationship, one must make a conscious decision either Conflict Resolution or Damage Control? Do you fix the problem as soon as it becomes a problem or do you wait and try and clean up the mess?

Dealing with conflict is something all of us must master simple because conflict is unavoidable. As long as each of us are individuals, we will always have different opinions, thoughts, and things that are important to each of us. So with this we welcome conflict. Understanding how to deal with conflict is very crucial to both your business and personal life. One bad apple definitely spoils the bunch. One bad experience and the repercussions can be devastating: professionally, personally and financially.

People talk. Especially about bad experiences. Conflict is not something you can ignore and expect it to get better.

So how do we handle conflict? With respect, of course. During conflict resolution, you must respect the other person's needs while resolving the problem. You must figure out a way to make the situation a "win/win" for all parties involved in order to salvage or maintain the relationship.

Conflict is not something you can ignore and it will get better. I explain in greater detail how confrontation actually works.

And what is my next point? Of course respect. Here during conflict resolution you must respect the other person's needs while resolving the conflict.

Control is another point I could stay on forever. One most important thing everyone must understand is that you are the only person you can control so…CONTROL YOURSELF! PERIOD! Out of ten people there may have be four different personality types, so you must learn how to control yourself with each personality.

Everyone has the potential to get upset and even angry, especially when there is a difference of opinion. So it is up to you to keep all tempers in check, especially yours. To control the situation, you must first master controlling yourself.

Hey, I know I may sound a bit redundant but here is the respect factor once again. When you learn how to control yourself you are unconsciously displaying respect for the other person.

Finally, the last ingredient in building a solid relationship is consistency. The reason I decided to make this point last is because it ties up everything that was stated. Do the steps, repeat, and then keep doing them. When you are dealing with other people, especially difficult people, it is VERY easy to just try to deal with them then walk away when it feels like it's not working. You will never know without giving it the proper attention and time. Whatever you water will grow. Water your relationships and they will grow. Ignore them and they will die. You can already guess yes, respect plays in here as well. Respect yourself to become consistent in your relationships, this is what builds character.

Respect is the main ingredient to every relationship. If there is no respect on even one person's behalf, then the relationship cannot last and will ultimately die.

To build on a relationship, each person involved must maintain a level of respect for the other. A relationship with no respect is like a house built on sand, it is unstable and it will keep sinking until it is gone.

CHAPTER FIVE
SELF-AWARENESS

"To say "I love you" one must know first how to say the "I"."

--Ayn Rand

Who Am I?

The very first place you must start is asking yourself the question, "Who are you?" Think about it very deeply. Don't tell me what you do (for example, you may be a doctor, or a nurse, etc.). Tell me who you are. I will begin by telling you who I am. I am a woman who does NOT like to just jump out of bed and get my day started. I am also a woman who does NOT like loud annoying noises.

So knowing just these two things about myself, I know that I must set my alarm clock one hour before I have to get up and continue to hit the snooze button for the duration of that time. Why? Because the hour gives me time to take my time getting out of bed. But the annoying sound of the snooze button ensures that I don't take too much time because again I don't like hearing that noise so it's going to motivate me to get out of the bed and get a move on. See where I'm going with this?

What Do I Love To Do?

Just as you looked deeply inside to find who you are, look again and find what you love to do. I am the type of person who loves all things entertainment-related; therefore I love movies, music, art, and theatre. I could spend hours in these things and not so much as look up.

When Do I want to start?

Goal setting is one of the most liberating aspects of having a wonderful and fulfilling life. Not only with just setting goals but with writing them down and viewing them often. Don't worry if you feel like you are no good with goal setting, trust me I have been there. There is a saying that goes, "How do you eat an elephant? One bite at a time". So, when you are beginning the process of goal setting, start off small and working your way forward will help you achieve this with minimal frustrations.

For example, start by making a goal of whatever

it is that you would like to accomplish for that day and write it down. Once you get in the habit of setting goals, you will get better so you can then move to your weekly goals. Eventually you will look up and have met both short-term goals(within one year) and long-term goals (within two to five years).

Where Do I start?

This is the most simple of the steps, but most people want to complicate it. Start wherever you are. If you'd like to become the type of person who sets goals so that your life could have more meaning and purpose, start where you are with the daily goals. Let's say for the sake of argument that you need to run errands. Write down everything you need to do for that day and those are your goals. Then daily, make an intention to plan your days. Whatever you start to plan eventually becomes habit and whatever you can make a habit becomes a part of your life.

Why Am I Doing this?

Self-awareness is huge for becoming a people person because for you to read others and become the type of person that everyone considers the "go-to" person, you must become aware of who you are and who others are as well. When you know who you are, you become more self-aware of your actions and also the actions of others. You then begin to develop what most would call your "why"; that thing that drives you to do what you do.

How often do I do this?

Everyday. Remember consistency is key with any and everything that you want to be successful in life. Practice becoming self-aware in all aspects of life. Get to the point that you conduct what I like to call a "self-check" each and every time you even so much as have a conversation with another person. You want to be totally aware of how you are being perceived by others. This will hone your craft of becoming the most effective people person in the world.

"Trust is built with consistency." -- Lincoln Chafee

CHAPTER SIX

P-E-O-P-L-E Model

"People frequently point to communication as a problem, because it's easy to notice, but usually it is a symptom of an underlying problem with a relationship posture."
— Roberta Gilbert

Ok, now that we've got a fundamental understanding of relationships under our belt, let's move on to our main focus: developing your PEOPLE skills. For the sake of word play, we use the acronym PEOPLE to help you remember the main focus in the people person model.

Passion, Empathy, Observation, Participation, Listening, and **Empower** are what being a people person is all about.

Learn to listen to what people say. Sympathizing with someone will earn his or her trust and admiration. Really listen, not with your ears, but with your heart. Look the person in the eye and pay attention and let the person know that every word they say is important to you.

Do not be a fake. Hypocrites only know the way down. If you are genuinely nice to people and interested in them, people know that. People are not stupid and they will also know when you are a big fake and are only thinking of yourself. There is no power in fakery.

Be kind wherever and however you can. You do not have to be rich to be charitable. Just the little things matter more to others. Help your elderly neighbor in his yard. Volunteer at a nursing home if possible. Good deeds do not go out of style.

Find the joy in unrestrained laughter. Not the fake polite laugh when you really are not amused. Laughter attracts people and eventually success. Find the humor in every situation possible and try not to take things so seriously. That does not mean being a clown. Just be genuine and share your joy.

Remember that you also deserve to be valued. Being the life the party does not mean being a pushover. If you value yourself, others will as well. You are worthy of dignity and respect and people would rather be around someone who demands the same.

Never be arrogant. Showing confidence in yourself is attractive. Being arrogant will definitely not endear you to others. When you meet someone for the first time, put on that winning smile and show your confidence.

Always keep your temper in check. It is not cool to snap at someone when you are angry. Temper tantrums are unbecoming to a child, not to mention an adult. Turn your anger into something productive. If people think you are always ready to explode, you will not easily gain their confidence.

Keep people close. It is easy to get caught up in life and lose touch with people. With the technology available today, there is no excuse to remain apart from others. It has been said that people with lots of friends tend to live longer. That makes a lot of sense when you think about it. If you feel good and you feel supported, life is a lot better.

Don't be a grouch. Do you want to go through life as a grump? You will not grow personally as long as you carry these traits with you. Get rid of them. How much fun are you to be around?

Relationships wither without care and nurturing. No matter what happens, you must keep those relationships with your family and friends alive.

These are the people who matter the most, so make sure to have some fun together. Joy will never be far away so long as these significant people are kept close.

Passion

Have you ever attended a meeting, speech, workshop or any type of gathering where the speaker simply stood up, walked to the podium and started talking? With few or no notes, they held you transfixed and spellbound throughout their entire presentation?

Has anyone ever asked you a question and you began to speak and the conversation just started to flow? Time just seemed to fly!

Passion is defined as an intense, driving, or overmastering feeling or conviction; strong or ardent affection such as love or hate; a strong liking or desire for or devotion to some activity, object, or concept. What "lights your fire" is considered your passion!

Usually when we speak of "passion", all thoughts turn to the romantic or sexual type of passion. This isn't necessarily a bad thing, because all it shows is that a person thinks or feels strongly about another. But for today's purpose, we will be discussing the type of passion that drives you!

The first thing anyone should see when they meet you is your passion! They should be able to see the fire that burns from within you. What excites you to no avail? Is it the fact that you are a stay-at-home Mom or

Dad dedicated to your children? How about because you are living out your dream of making money while doing the thing that you love?

For me, I love people, so the fact that I can teach people how to be a confident leader like myself, EXCITES ME! Whatever it is, people need to see this!

Have you ever wondered why people fall in by the droves to Wal-Mart Stores? It's very simple. Passion. I did a study on Wal-Mart Company and I understand why they can continue to hire people even during a recession. What is the first thing you see when you walk into any Wal-Mart Stores? A door greeter. Wal-Mart gets it. Wal-Mart had a brilliant idea of asking their customers what they wanted and what would make them feel more welcome to come into their stores. It took just a simple statement from a customer to say that it would be nice to see a friendly face when you walked in. This is how the concept of a door greeter was inspired and the brilliance began. Something about seeing a friendly face when you first walk into the store is what really makes the experience great.

Wal-Mart is not losing any money even in this tough economy because they have adopted the principle of people passionate about greeting people. Some people say even if they don't have any money they will go to Wal-Mart. So simply by adopting the principle of having passion when meeting others will take your business a long way.

Can you think of some other companies that inspire a passionate response?

Who are they?

Why or how do they inspire passion?

Empathy

I would LOVE to teach an entire class on this subject! However, for the sake of time, we will condense this down to just what needs to be addressed. The very meaning of empathy is simple: It is the action of understanding, being aware of or being sensitive to experiencing the feelings and thoughts of someone else.

Much like compassion, empathy is feeling what someone else is feeling or has gone through.

Back to that saying: "People don't care how much you know until they know how much you care." So what does this really mean? It means the more you empathize with others the stronger your connection will be with them; therefore, the better your communication will be.

Empathy begins relationships and relationships stem from communication. When you communicate effectively with someone, they want to communicate with you more.

One important fact that you should always keep in mind is that you don't always have to agree with the other person's feelings, opinions or persona, but trying to understand where they are coming from gives you a leg up. It gives you additional insight into what makes that person tick. What drives them?

What makes them the kind of person that they are? Empathy can be one of the most powerful 'people tools' in your arsenal.

Understand that difficult people usually come from one of three places: fear, insecurity, or anger.

Fear- "I'm afraid that I don't really know what I'm doing and someone will find out."

Insecurity- "I'm afraid that I'm not really good enough or worthy of dealing with all of this!"

Anger- "Why am I always THE one having to handle things?"
(Anger can also be a very tricky one to deal with because the person rarely realizes that the anger is there! And many times when we're faced with anger, we tend to get defensive really quickly!) Recognize it for what it is… There is nothing that YOU have done to make this person angry! Take

a deep breath, keep your cool, smile sincerely and move on.

It is also important to keep in mind that having empathy for someone does NOT mean that you have to be a sucker for them! Simply recognize what the real issue is and use that information to your benefit.

This is all about working smarter not harder. If I can sincerely understand and relate to you, there is nothing that you won't do for me, simply because you like me and WANT to do it.

Being in business means that the one thing that most people understand is "Sell, sell, sell!" That should not be your driving force. Discard this thought for a moment please. If you can truly empathize with a person and they realize it, you can sell ice to an Eskimo in the middle of a blizzard, or, better yet, a refrigerator!

Observation

This is exactly what it means, to pay careful attention to or to keep a watchful eye. What is it that you need to observe? Body language, if you are in a face to face situation.

Actions speak louder than words, especially when you are dealing with someone who finds it difficult to communicate. You must rely on your powers of observation in order to be proactive in the relationship-building process.

Most people were blessed with two eyes, two ears and one mouth for a very important reason. You must watch and listen twice as much as you speak! One thing that I have noticed about being a speaker is that when I am speaking, it is VERY difficult to listen. So if you know this is the truth, you can use this to your advantage when you're first meeting someone and just getting to know them.

If you observe their behavior, you can use those cues and learn how to relate to them. For example, if you notice that a person constantly interrupts you when you speak, this could mean several things:

(a) It could mean is that this is a very impatient person so you must practice patience with them in order to relate to them.

(b) It could also mean that this person likes to be in control. So you may have to reassure them (discreetly and indirectly) that they are in control

of their portion of the relationship so
that you can move forward.

(c) It may also mean that you have
to ask more directed questions to get
a straightforward, informative
answer.

(d) Or they could simply be
nervous! It's up to you to discover,
discern and decide!

Observation is one of your greatest
assets as a people person. Hone your
skills and learn to "read" people!
Watch the person as you hold a
conversation with them. Do their
words match their actions? Why or
why not? Do they maintain eye
contact as you converse? Are they

calm or nervous and fidgety? Glance around the room, what does this environment say about them? Through practice, you will learn to refine your observation skills and to trust your judgment. FYI: It only takes about 5 minutes to observe someone's behavior!

Normally you see only what you want to see. Your selective attention severely limits your ability to reach your full observatory potential. Let me demonstrate. Imagine a penny, a 1 cent piece, in your mind. You have handled one thousands of times. Now, which way does Lincoln's profile face? Now take one out of your pocket and have a look. Chances are pretty good that you were wrong. Your range of observation is wide, but it almost always depends on your need to know. Which way Lincoln's face faces is pretty low on your need-to-know list.

The secret of using observation as a powerful tool is to train yourself. That's right, you can indeed teach yourself to see with new eyes every day—often in a situation where someone might want to tell a lie and you want to detect it.

Just as you can enhance your physical health with regular exercise, you can sharpen your powers of observation. For starters, watch people while they're talking. Practice studying people in conversation everywhere—at work, at a party, in a restaurant, on a plane or in the park. What you are looking for are the variations possible in different mannerisms or silent signals. You may even experiment by watching television with the sound off (actually not a bad idea to do all the time).

How many kinds of smiles do you see, and how would you evaluate them? How about frowns, smirks, finger pointing, dry coughs, and toe tapping? Observe mannerisms and try to assess the situation. What is the other person doing and why? Don't be afraid to ask why they did something either.

Soon you will become a collector of mannerisms. Quite frankly, it's not only easy, but there is a considerable amount of stimulating entertainment in putting the behavior of others under your own private magnifying glass. As a side benefit, you also become more sensitive to those around you.

Gradually, your increased observational abilities will pay off. In a week, you will be considerably more observant than you are today. After two weeks you'll be alert to nuances that seem elusive now.

In a month, with little effort, you'll be so observant that others will think you have some sort of super powers! You will be able to pick up on each of the mannerisms sent almost constantly both by friends and strangers.

The extent to which you can 'read' someone is determined by how many layers you're able to get them to reveal. And here's a little secret: a person will reveal their layers in direct proportion to you revealing yours. This is the onion theory in a nutshell.

Participation

This step is a little different because you must participate in your portion of the relationship. After you have observed the other person's behavior, you must actively participate to build the relationship.

Let me tell you a story. There was a young man who seemed very quiet. Although he was not shy, he never initiated a conversation. There was a young woman who noticed this about him and she began to approach him on the subject. "I used to think you were a shy man until I began to know you. You never walk up to anyone and start a conversation. You always wait until someone comes over to you before you speak. Why do you do this?" the young woman asked.

After a very surprised chuckle, the young man began to explain. "When I was younger, my mother always taught me to be respectful. She told me that it is very impolite to start a conversation. I never want to disrespect anyone, so I wait until they want to say something to me, and then I continue with the conversation."

If the young woman had not practiced the art of observation, she would never have been able to ask the very effective "why" question and may have even assumed the worst about this very respectful young man. So not only did she observe but she participated in her portion of the relationship by engaging his reasoning.

Think back to our discussion on EMPATHY. Understanding and empathizing with a person helps you to become a participant in the relationship. And in order to form a productive relationship, you must participate. You must actively join in. Why is it important to participate in a relationship? List some ways you can enhance your relationships.

Listening

One of my favorite steps—listening! This is by far the most IMPORTANT step to becoming a people person because if you are not listening then you are not learning.

Let's try this again; if you're not listening, you're not learning!

Learning about another individual is crucial to the growth and stability of any relationship. It is only when you master the art of listening that you can define the line between a close friend and someone who is just an associate.

Just as in the case of observing, listening to someone can tell you a lot about a person. When you observe someone, you watch to see if their words and actions complement each other. When you truly listen to a person, you learn to hear what IS being said and also what is NOT being said—which, at times, can be just as important! You hear the tone, the attitude, the "vibe" and, yes, even the passion of a person.

One of the most important things you must remember in listening to people is to LISTEN. Your goal is not to mentally prepare your next response, but to hear exactly what the person is trying to tell you. You are listening in order to carefully form a 'next question' that will fill in the gaps or give you further insight.

You must be an active listener. From time to time, repeat what the person has said—paraphrase it. This will let the speaker know that you are hearing them and, even more importantly, you understand what they are saying. If you can even include something of what they are NOT saying, they will look upon you in awe and wonder thinking that you are a genius! A mind-reader even!

You will begin to notice that, as you learn to listen carefully, you will have insight into the person's next move. This is simply because you have taken the time to listen and learn them. Always keep in mind the vision of two ears and one mouth.

Remember to listen twice as much as you speak!

Empower

The final step of this process is empowerment. Empowerment can only happen once you have finally become that 'people person'. Once you have fine-tuned your skills and have become comfortable with your abilities you can empower others.

When your people skills are all working together, others want to be around you. They want to be like you. They want you to become a part of their inner circle. This is the reason all other steps that have come before are so vital. When you listen and learn about another individual, you can pinpoint what you have to offer them in the relationship and therefore spend your time enhancing what will make you more effective.

Empowering an individual is another very important step in interpersonal relations skills. If someone feels they have no power or control over their life in your relationship, they will soon end it. This is where you find high employee turnover rates and low morale.

It is important to understand that empowerment is not about giving people power, but helping people to recognize and use their own powers.

It encourages people to gain skills, knowledge and confidence that will allow them to overcome obstacles in their own lives or work environment to become the best that they can be!

Ultimately, the empowerment step is about giving back. Helping others to realize their power and encouraging them to be their best is what being a 'people person' is all about!

CHAPTER SEVEN
RESPONSIBLE THINKING

"You must take personal responsibility. You cannot change the circumstances, the seasons, or the wind, but you can change yourself. That is something you have charge of." – Jim Rohn

The key to building strong and lasting relationships is to spend quality time together. Quality time is that kind of time that is interactive, such as taking a walk, playing a game, singing karaoke (my personal favorite) or working on a project together. What that time together does is build sufficient relational strength into the relationship. This means that, when you have disagreements or an argument, there is adequate strength in the relationship to help you rise above your differences, set the other person as your No. 1 priority, rise above the unhappy feelings, and work things out.

Always get into the habit of getting a buy-in from others instead of telling them what to do. Cooperation works much better than getting someone to be compliant. Think about it this way, who is doing the thinking when you tell people what to do? You have to ask what they think or what they are doing. I did a study once with my children, weighing the productivity of cooperation (a.k.a. buy-in) versus compliance (a.k.a. punishment) and the results were amazing.

Imagine a parenting discipline program that actually teaches children to take responsibility for their own behavior without trying to control them or do something to them to make them change their behavior. And imagine a discipline program where there are no rewards, no special treats, and no punishment. Yes, no punishment. No predetermined time for time-outs or spanking. And the children decide the amount of time required for chores or what type of discipline to receive for not following the rules.

And yet, the results of this study provided remarkable results in improved discipline throughout the home. There were reductions in time-outs and misbehavior, and the parent had more time to teach the children with fewer frustrations. The success of this process has proven to shock me so greatly that I even tried it on a toddler, and if it worked on her then it will work for anyone. So how does it work? Let me explain.

One day, my toddler wanted to help her sister bake some banana bread for me. The reason she wanted to bake me something is because she heard on one of her cartoons a song that said something about, "making something for someone else shows that I love you," so in her little mind, she wanted to show her mommy that she loved me.

So we went shopping for all the items needed to make her wonderful banana bread. She and her sister got in the kitchen and began to mix the ingredients and everything else that was needed to ensure this banana bread turned out well. Once all items were mixed and in the pan, my oldest daughter put the pan in the oven to bake. My toddler would check often on the progress of the banana bread until it was finally complete.

When my oldest daughter took the baked beauty out of the oven, she told my toddler that she could not touch it because it had to cool off first. Well, this did not go over well with the little lady and she stomped out of the kitchen, into her room and slammed her door closed. Hearing the commotion, I immediately called her into the family room so that I could speak with her.

I simply asked her, "Why did you stomp out and slam the door?" With her hands folded across her chest and an angry scowl on her face, she said, "Because my sister just made me so mad." I asked another question. "What did your sister do that made you so mad?" She looked at me almost like "duh" and said, "She don't let me touch the banana bread."

I sat her down and explained to her that being angry sometimes happens and I am glad that she was able to express her feelings. But I also wanted to help her learn how to express them better and feel better at the same time. I told her, "When you get angry, count to ten then talk about it and you will feel better." So I said, "Let's try it now." As she counted to ten, I begin to make silly faces and by the time she got to ten, she burst into laughter and said, "I feel better now."

She went quietly into the kitchen, asked her sister how long it would be before she could touch the banana bread and all was well. The moral of the story is learn how to think more responsibly and your social skills will improve. Instead of me yelling at my daughter and telling her NOT to slam doors and stomp in the house, I taught her how to think more responsibly. Once she learned how to manage her emotions, SHE made the decision to act in a more appropriate manner.

Emotions can either be your master or your slave; either you will control them or they, most definitely, will control you. When you learn to control your emotions in all situations, you learn how to think responsibility and, in turn, it helps you become a better people person.

When you monitor your own behavior by taking responsibility for what you do, this is when you become more of a people magnet.

Being able to control yourself is a very attractive trait because, sadly, the majority of people do not possess this strength. Once you become a responsible thinker, you begin to display this to others. You begin to ask them what they think about situations. In turn, you are allowing them to own their feelings, take responsibility, and empower themselves at the same time. Can you say confident leader?

Punishment and rewards do not teach people to think, they are only a method of control. We are not designed to be controlled. Maybe if we taught others how to think more responsibly then the prisons would not be so overcrowded, but I digress (smile). Being a people person through responsible thinking is a process that teaches respect for others.

People people are the ones who can make a huge difference in the world and help make it a better place—by simply helping to promote positive change within others. What can bring about a growing belief in others that they are able to make things better for themselves? What promotes change within another person, and what makes change possible?

First, it is the belief that someone cares, that someone really respects you and is willing to work with you until you can succeed. Second, it is the belief that somehow it is possible to succeed, to make things better, and to resolve our internal conflicts.

If properly applied, you as a people person begin to develop a sense of responsibility for your own life and to respect the lives of everyone around you.

In order to understand how to think more responsibly, you must understand what you think about— or, in other words, think about what you're thinking about. "Watch your thoughts; they become words. Watch your words; they become actions. Watch your actions; they become habit. Watch your habits; they become character. Watch your character; it becomes your destiny."
– Lao Tzu

So begin to watch what you hold on to in your mental space, because you will eventually begin to act on whatever it is that is deeply ingrained in your mind.

We create our life with our thoughts and with our words. The words we speak and the thoughts we think have great power in the way our life unfolds. The quality and form of our thoughts and words have a direct impact on the quality and form of our life experiences.

You can choose to be happy or unhappy; the operative word here is choice. Why not choose to make a habit of healthy thoughts and words? Warren Felt Evans **coined the phrase, "thoughts are things**." He meant that thoughts and words carry energy and intention with them that have specific and predictable results in the physical universe. When you think great things, you begin to attract great things.

Thoughts magnetically attract similar energies that collect until they become the physical and emotional life that you feel and live.

What becomes of your life? The physical, mental, emotional, biochemical and medical results you experience spring directly from the thoughts and words you use to tell yourself what is and what isn't true for you. Your physical life is all about what's happening in your mind, because it happens there first. You tell yourself the story of your life and then you live it. Are you telling yourself the kind of story you want to be telling yourself? Are you having the kind of life experiences you want to be having? Are your habits of mind and BODY positive habits?

Every minute of every day, you are creating your life. Are you consciously creating the life you want or are you creating your life purely by force of habit? To create the life you really want, learn about FORCE OF HABIT and TRANSFORMATION. Find out how it works and make it work for you. You're the only one who can do it.

Ways of thinking more responsibly

Pay attention to your community. Look for genuine ways to demonstrate responsibility. You don't need to volunteer to pick up trash at a park or to help at a local animal shelter in order to be a responsible citizen. Even putting your soda can in the recycling bin or picking up a piece of garbage you dropped demonstrate responsible behavior.

Spend some time thinking about your own needs and desires. Focus on something specific you want and consider how to achieve that goal responsibly. Think of other people in your life who exhibit good examples of responsible behavior and planning and consider ways you can become more like them. When you spend time consciously thinking about responsibility, you will learn to unintentionally think responsibly.

Educate yourself on issues in your community. One of the most important ways you can be responsible is to know what issues directly affect you and your neighbors. If you understand what your local problems are, you will be better equipped to face those issues. Read your newspaper, attend local meetings and talk to people in your community to find out what's going on and what ways you can help your neighborhood become a better, safer place in which to live.

This book is dedicated to helping you to get as much benefit and enjoyment out of life as possible. In order to learn how to increase your influence, you must first learn the steps of being a people person.

"Give me six hours to chop down a tree and I will spend the first four sharpening the axe." – Abraham Lincoln

This is a wonderful quote because, to achieve the highest productivity, learning how to prioritize your work is what will help you to move ahead. As I have shown you through numerous examples of being a people person in this book, you will find that your natural attraction to others will catapult your business and/or personal life into space. At that point, you will realize that there is NOTHING you will not be able to accomplish.

CHAPTER EIGHT

CONSISTENCY

"We are what we repeatedly do. Excellence, then, is not an act, but a habit." – Aristotle

Ever heard the saying, "Sow a thought, reap an action; sow an action, reap a habit; sow a habit, reap a character; sow a character, reap a destiny"? This is very true. Everything we think about has consequences, as we spoke about in the previous chapter. Learning how to combine everything you learn and remain consistent with it will help to keep you in the confident leader category.

As I mentioned in a previous chapter, teaching children from a young age about the importance of developing healthy relationships and also understanding good social skills is very important. It fosters consistency in the social skills building process as well. It's never too early and kids are never too young to begin to build consistent relationships. Women can actually start to do this while a baby is in utero. Kids can actually identify the touch, smell, and voice of their parents when they're born.

The reason the one-on-one relationship is so important is because that's really how you begin to build basic trust. It's how kids learn how they can begin to trust you. One-on-one situations help kids learn who you are and how you react in situation after situation. Kids can't learn how to socialize with other children until they learn and know what a relationship is.

There are three primary ways to keep relationships going: eye contact, touching, and talking. Eye contact is such an engaging thing and it makes others feel like someone really wants to understand and have a relationship with them. With touching, something as simple as a handshake, hug or a pat on the shoulder sends a message that you really want to get to know the person. In talking, remember to allow the other person to talk twice as much as you—getting to know more about them as opposed to you doing all the talking.

Something that everyone has a need for in this world is feeling loved. This is true no matter what race, gender, or religion you are—everyone wants to feel loved. Seeing how this is something we all share, devote your time and energy to being consistently loving towards others.

Will there ever be a time when you, as a people person, will NOT like to express love towards others? Absolutely. This is when you learn how to spend some time doing nothing for no one so that you can remain in proper balance. Think about a glass.

When you have a glass with some liquid it in and you begin to pour it out, what happens to the liquid? Unless you are a magician, the liquid leaves the glass and you have nothing left. Only when you refill the glass again will you have more liquid to pour out again, if you so choose to. Think of yourself like the glass. If you have given everything you can give to others during the waking hours of your life, if you do not refill your glass, how can you have more to give?

In order to be happy as a people person, you must learn when to spend time with others and also when to spend time alone for refilling. When you think about others, spending time alone does not become about being selfish and self-centered, but more about reflecting on what happened during the day and how you as a person could be better.

Think about the universal goal once again. Most people not only want but NEED to feel loved and wanted in order to be happy. So being a people person wires you to become highly motivated to learn and practice loving others more consistently. Many people do so initially, but do not sustain their skills for the duration of a long-term relationship-building process.

Being loving, attentive, other-centered, caring, and admiring of others comes naturally during the initial stage of most relationships. As time progresses, there is a reduction in these "feelings", especially if and when someone disappoints you to the point of hurting your feelings.

This is something that we must fight hard to resist. It is human nature to be egotistical, where you are only looking out for your own feelings and best interests. But learning how to love and accept others for who they are is something that you will have to adapt to when becoming a people person.

You can only practice doing this through being consistent. If you are developing a relationship with someone, whether friendship or otherwise, you must practice doing

what is difficult over and over again
in order to make it habit.

We need to learn what works and
repeat it long enough for it to
become a behavioral habit. Though it
is said that "practice makes perfect",
this is not true. Some would even
argue that practice does not make
perfect, but it does make it habit. So
practice being consistent so that it
becomes a habit.

Practicing loving behaviors is a
must—from meeting someone for
the first time to meeting with
someone on a weekly basis. Relaxing
our expressions of appreciation,

caring, admiration, loving acts, affection, passion, support and true friendship are grave errors of neglect that may reduce the happiness quotient within any relationship.

Remember that you already have all the skills needed to attract, give, and receive love. Practice your commitment to others; the key is just to become consistent with it. Recognize that love is reciprocal. If you feel less than thrilled about the love you receive, assess your own loving conduct.

Practice loving behaviors on a daily basis. The repetition of providing attention, communication, and teamwork makes them habitual and comforting. Know that feeling loved is the greatest gift you could ever give anyone. Give freely and often to others. Help others feel valued and desired. It is likely to promote reciprocity and create a blissful relationship with others.

Don't underestimate the importance of consistency. It is the difference between having tea with someone tomorrow and them boosting your career by promoting you instead of you having to do all the hard work yourself.

I recently asked some Facebook friends to provide one word only that describes me and guess what I found out. MOST of the people chose the word consistent. It was great to see what others truly thought about me. Learning how to be consistent in relationship-building is huge in order to gain trust from anyone. Others need to understand that you are who you say you are. So be you and be consistent.

Do what you say you are going to do and treat people the same way no matter what is the best advice I have ever learned as a people person. Even when I meet mean people, if they are always mean, at least I know that I can count on them to be mean. Lack of consistency can kill a relationship.

Years ago, when I worked for a hospital, I used to read every morning in the break room and leave my reading on the table in case others wanted to read. Day after day I did this like clockwork. I never heard anyone ever saying anything about the reading on the table so, one day, after I completed my daily reading, I tossed it in the trash, thinking to myself, *No one reads this except me anyway so why clutter up the table?* Lunchtime came; the break room was unusually crowded that particular day. As I sat down to eat, I overheard a couple of women talking and could not help but notice on particular conversation. These women were talking and a young lady got up from the table obviously looking for something.

"What are you looking for?" asked one of the ladies.

"I am looking for the daily reading that usually someone leaves on the table. It is always interesting and I thought maybe someone misplaced it because it is no longer on the table."

I cannot begin to tell you how badly I felt when I heard her say that. Needless to say, I never threw away the reading anymore after that.

Moral of the story is even when you don't think someone else is watching, please understand they are. Sometimes people are silent about their need for your consistency, so continue to love others, become more people-focused and be consistent, someone else may be counting on you.

Just like the woman in the story, people will feel cheated if you started being one way then change up on them. One of the things you don't want others to feel about you is that you only do what you need to do to get where you need to be. That, in a word, is called manipulation.

Keep in mind that relationships are intricate, and actions always cause reactions. If we stop doing the things that others appreciated or relied on, we should expect a negative reaction.

Below are a few key tips to ensure consistency in your relationships.

Don't start behavior patterns that you can't maintain. If you can't keep it up, don't set the expectation.

Don't pretend to love anything that falls outside of the realm of your natural behavior. If you don't enjoy karaoke, don't tell someone you do in order to gain a friendship. Let them know that this isn't something you normally would do but that you are participating because you want to understand them better. Never be deceptive.

Understand what other people like, and if this is something that doesn't go against who you are, keep doing those things. If they're things that you do not enjoy, simply say it and move forward. At least you will always be honest in the process.

Don't slack off! Maintenance is the key to a successful relationship and I cannot stress this enough. Sometimes life gets in the way. You may slack off at times but continue to keep the communication open so that others will not feel slighted.

If you ever wanted to know what glue holds a people person together, that glue would be consistency. Without it, you are merely a manipulator looking for your next victim. Most people will be able to see right through you. Eventually others will speak of you in a negative light and all of your efforts will be for naught.

So if there is anything you could take away with you from this book, please take how to truly love and respect others for who they are, treat them as such and be consistent in doing so. If you follow these steps, you are guaranteed to not only make a huge difference in the world but also get 100% of what you want in life!

CHAPTER NINE
CONFIDENT LEADER SKILLS

There is nothing more important in being an effective leader than having self-confidence. A leader makes the hard calls. A leader challenges their teams to reach and achieve above and beyond their comfort levels. You can have the best communication skills and be an amazing people person, but without confidence, you are standing on sinking sand. Why? Because CONFIDENCE is the foundation on which everything else is built. If you are not confident in your ability to lead then you are nothing more than a manager.

Collaborative, Organized, Nurturing, Fearless, Integrity, Direct, Encouraging, Natural, and Transparent are the skills we will focus on to close the chapter on being a confident leader.

Collaborative

A "CONFIDENT Leader" must be able to work past their own ego. To work collaboratively, a leader must include various stakeholders in order to work towards a beneficial solution for all involved and be able to share knowledge and credit. Being a collaborative leader means being able to have the vision to bring in a coalition of groups that will bring different ideas on how to address the problem.   A strong leader welcomes the diversity of opinions and encourages the input of the group to make decisions and then allows everyone to share in the credit.

Organized

Organized leaders build confidence. When the leader is organized they create a sense of purpose, focus and order that gives a sense of credibility. A confident team has a competitive advantage because it is not wasting energy trying to make sense out of chaos. An organized leader has a way of making the team's purpose clear and, more importantly, doable.

An organized leader sets the bar for their team's expectation. The team knows what is expected of them and they are able to follow through and deliver outstanding results when completing the tasks.

Nurturing

When the term "nurturing" is mentioned, most thoughts go towards "mothering or caring for something". It sounds like a foreign word to the world of business. However, nurturing can be one of the most productive practices of a Confident Leader! A nurturing leader recognizes the 'hidden' and undiscovered leaders within their own organization.   That effective leader gives them the encouragement and opportunities to grow, develop and become highly effective leaders in their own right.

Fearless

If you adhere to the myth of the "Fearless Leader", you will probably think in terms of a chest pounding male who considers himself 'the leader of the pack' and is always ready to jump head first into new adventures. The truth is far from that thought. The truth is that you could probably not find a single leader who does not experience a deep fear … especially of failing. However, truly fearless leaders overcome that fear by facing it and analyzing the risks and putting plans in place for the best favorable outcome. They do not let fear overcome them; they look the fear in the face and make choices about how to make that fear work for them.

Integrity

Integrity is the character trait that builds trust between people. It can be said that integrity is doing the right thing when no one is looking. Integrity comes from former experiences of a moral slant. As a leader, in order to garner the respect of your team it is important not only to have integrity but to seek it out in others. A leader with integrity always looks for the best in their teams, pursuing what is good in them. That special leader does things for his/her team with their best interests in mind. It is always about the good of the team and not just the leader.

Integrity means a deep commitment to doing the right thing for the right reason, no matter the circumstance. People who have integrity are usually considered incapable of breaking the trust of those who have confided in them. Choosing the right thing, no matter what the consequence, is a true sign of integrity.

Direct

Direct leadership is characterized as a leader who tells his/her immediate staff what to do and how they are expected to perform the given tasks. While direct leadership may not the best way to lead in a long-term manner, it does work well when the team is unfamiliar with the new task at hand. A Confident Leader knows when to be direct and when to delegate.

Encouraging

The importance of encouragement is often overlooked because it is usually done in private. A Confident Leader understands and knows the importance of encouraging their team. People want to be appreciated and acknowledged. Encouraging them in public, as well as in private, gives them motivation and courage to work even harder.

According to the Webster dictionary, encouragement is defined as the act of inspiring others with renewed courage, renewed spirit or renewed hope.

"Humans need encouragement as much as plants need water. We constantly encourage or discourage those around us and thereby contribute materially to their greater or lesser ability to function."
Rudolf Dreikurs

Natural

All too often, the loud, brassy, take charge person is considered to be a natural leader. That is not always the case! Loud does not equal leading. A natural leader sees the whole picture, makes calculated decisions and gets the team to move in his/her direction and makes things happen.

Confident leadership isn't just about sitting at the top of the corporate ladder and running the show. It is about engaging your social network, community, colleagues and employees to share a vision and unite people in pursuit of a common goal. A natural leader knows how to bring out the qualities of everyone around them.

Transparent

There is one leadership characteristic that commonly gets overlooked. However, it can be the most important characteristic if you truly want to be considered a Confident Leader. That one characteristic is transparency. Transparency means that you, as the leader, are open and honest. Your team puts their trust in you because they know that you will give true feedback.

What are some of the benefits of transparency to a Confident Leader? Healthy, professional relationships develop. People trust you and that creates a cohesive and safe workplace environment. Problems are solved much easier because opinions are valued and respectfully discussed. The teams are willing to work together to find solutions as fast as possible. They understand that it is a joint effort. Not surprisingly, the teams work harder and more productively.

SPECIAL BONUS OFFER
CONFIDENT LEADER
SEMINAR FREE!

As a thank you for purchasing *The Confident Leader,* I am offering a scholarship for you and a family member or friend to attend the one-day Confident Leader Seminar as my guest. That is a total value of $300 for free! Also, you get a FREE People Person assessment (P-PAC) at www.beaconfidentleader.com.

These guest seats are available to purchasers of *The Confident Leader* as a way of saying thank you and to assist in helping you become more confident for a better life. All seating is first come, first served. To assure your spot, please register immediately at www.beaconfidentleader.com.

At the Confident Leader seminar, you will expand upon the insights provided in this book by taking action to:

- Find and express your passion.
- Learn empathy through exercises.
- Put observation into practice.
- Participate in conversations to win people.
- Practice the art of listening.

- Ultimately implement all action steps to empower others.

By the end of the seminar, you will have the inner capacity to build productive relationships that will lead to increasing your influence. Best part about it, the same inner strategies that you will learn will enhance your inner peace and happiness as well. Can you say win-win?

Whether you are someone who considers yourself a people person, would like to brush up on your people skills or just don't get people at all, register for the Confident

Leader Seminar today. This seminar will change your life because I will show you all the secrets and tips you need to know in order to become a confident leader and relate to any person on any level! Register now at www.beaconfidentleader.com

After reading the book, sign up for my FREE Confident Leader™ Seminar and "Like" us on Facebook https://www.facebook.com/TamekaAndersonWilliams/. Browse around to find all kinds of free resources and pictures. Also tell us how this book helped you by dropping a comment and letting others know your intention to become a more confident leader.

37434324R00137

Made in the USA
San Bernardino, CA
18 August 2016